The Colle...

by Norman Sch...

THE CAST

SAM

MOUSE

JOJO

BEN

MELANIE
a new member
of the class

MR HOPKINS
class teacher
for the day

MRS TURNER
the head teacher

Scene 1

The classroom at Story Street Primary School. Everyone is rushing to finish setting out a display of objects that they have brought in to school.

MR HOPKINS Two minutes everyone! I'd like you to have your collections displayed by playtime. Then we can look at them when we come back in.

JOJO *(Searching in her bag)* Come on, where is it?

MOUSE Hey, mind you don't knock my space models over!

JOJO Well, if you didn't take up the whole table, then maybe I'd have a whole ten square centimetres to display my collection!

BEN *(Pointing at the felt-tip pens pot)* Pass me the red, I want to underline my caption cards.

MOUSE Do we have to make caption cards?

SAM Of course we do, otherwise no one will know what the objects are.

MOUSE But everyone knows what this is. It's my space collection.

SAM Yeah, but see how I've written about my wildlife collection.

MOUSE	So what?
BEN	Mr Hopkins did say he wanted it to look like a museum display.
JOJO	There! I've finished.
BEN	Hey, really eye-catching!
SAM	Oh, I really like it!
MOUSE	*(Laughing)* Yeah, nearly as good as mine! *They all laugh.*
BEN	Where did you get all these football programmes from?
JOJO	My dad said I could have his collection ages ago. And this lot here *(pointing to a group of programmes)* are all Wellbridge United programmes. I'm a Junior Member.
SAM	*(Pointing at the programme in the middle)* Why's this one covered in a plastic jacket?
JOJO	Because this is my best one – the 1966 World Cup Final: England versus West Germany.
MR HOPKINS	Wow! 4–2 to England! I remember watching England winning the World Cup on our black and white telly when I was a lad. How did you get the programme, Jojo?

JOJO If you read the caption, Mr Hopkins …

MR HOPKINS *(Reading the caption card)* 'My dad's uncle gave me this programme. He was a ballboy during the tournament.' I'm impressed! Well, full of envy really. Your dad's uncle was actually there when Geoff Hurst banged in the winning goal! *(Pretending he is the TV commentator)* 'Some people are on the pitch! They think it's all over … Well it is now!'

MOUSE	*(Confused)* What's all over?
MR HOPKINS	Your time for doing displays. *(Loudly)* Please stop what you're doing everybody and sit down by your display. *They all stop working and sit down.*
MOUSE	But I haven't finished.
BEN	Can I stay in with Mouse at playtime to help him finish his caption cards, Mr Hopkins?
MOUSE	*(Looking hopeful)* Thanks, Ben.
MR HOPKINS	I'm sorry boys, I'm afraid you can't. I can't supervise you. I'm seeing Mrs Turner at playtime.
SAM	*(Joking)* Have you been naughty Mr Hopkins?
MR HOPKINS	*(Joining in with the joke and pretending to look glum)* Yes, Mrs Turner wants to know why I wrote all over the board this morning.
MOUSE	But, you're allowed to write on the board. You're a teacher!
JOJO	It's a joke, Mouse. Sometimes your ability to miss the point amazes me!

MOUSE   *(Ignoring his sister)* Oh pleeease, can I stay in to finish, Mr Hopkins?

MR HOPKINS   Sorry, Mouse, I just …

BEN   We can take paper and stuff and do it outside.

MR HOPKINS   There! A perfect solution to your problem!
Mrs Turner enters carrying an armful of folders. She has a girl with her. The girl is not wearing Story Street School uniform.

MRS TURNER Oh, I'm glad to have caught you before playtime. *(She puts her pile of folders down on Jojo and Mouse's table.)*

MOUSE *(Whispering to Sam)* You see, Hoppo *is* in trouble.

MRS TURNER I'd like to introduce Melanie. Melanie Parfitt. She was supposed to start with us tomorrow, but Melanie has arrived early and … and we're very pleased to have you, Melanie!

SAM *(Whispering to Jojo)* Oh good, another girl!

MRS TURNER *(To Melanie)* This is Mr Hopkins, your teacher for the day, and this is going to be your new class. They're a lovely lot. *(To the class)* So I'm sure there'll be lots of people who will look after Melanie and show her around.
Everyone puts their hand up to volunteer.

MR HOPKINS Welcome, Melanie. Well, as you can see, it's not a typical day. Everyone has brought in a collection of special things to display. Who can tell Mrs Turner and Melanie why we're doing this?
Everyone puts up their hand again. Mr Hopkins points to Ben.

BEN We're going to Wellbridge Museum next week. To help us understand how museums display collections of interesting things, we've brought in our own collections. Mine's about superheroes!

JOJO I'm displaying my collection of football programmes.

SAM	My collection is called 'Save Our Wild Life'. I've got loads of things about endangered animals, especially turtles.
MOUSE	And mine's about space. I got my first rocket model when I was two and then I got this one *(pointing at a model)* when we went on holiday to … er … I can't remember where, but – *The bell sounds for playtime.*
MRS TURNER	Ah, saved by the bell!
MR HOPKINS	*(To Melanie)* We'll talk some more after playtime. Sam, will you and Jojo make Melanie feel at home and show her where everything is?
SAM **JOJO**	Yes, Mr Hopkins! *(They go up to Melanie and start to talk to her.)*

MR HOPKINS Do you still need to see me, Mrs Turner?

MRS TURNER Excuse me, Mouse. *(She picks up her pile of folders from the table.)* Yes, there are one or two things we need to discuss.

BEN *(Whispering to Mouse in a jokey way)* Oh, look, Hoppo *is* in trouble.

MOUSE *(Whispering to Ben in a serious voice)* I bet she makes Mr Hopkins clean the board!

BEN *(Raising his eyes in disbelief)* Oh, Mouse. You are so easy to fool!

Scene 2

Sam, Jojo and Melanie are in a quiet area of the playground.

MELANIE	Thanks for showing me round. It's much smaller than my old school.
JOJO	Why did you move school?
MELANIE	Mum's job.
JOJO	Oh. *Pause.*
SAM	So, what do you like to do?
MELANIE	Mmm … oh, the usual.
SAM	Jojo's really mad about football. I expect you don't like –
MELANIE	Are you? Is that why you've got all those football programmes?
SAM	*(Pretending to be bored)* Oh, no, not another football fanatic!
MELANIE	I really love football. I was in the school team in my old school.
JOJO	*(Excited)* We've got a team! I play in it!

Enter Mouse and Ben with paper and felt-tip pens.

MOUSE	It's too windy to write out here.
BEN	I'll hold the paper down while you write.
JOJO	You'll never get it done in time. The bell will go soon.
MOUSE	Stop interfering. I thought you were supposed to be showing … er … Melanie around.
JOJO	This is my brother, Melanie!
MELANIE	Your brother! You don't look alike.
MOUSE } **JOJO**	Thank goodness!

SAM *(To Melanie)* Have you got any brothers or sisters?

MELANIE No. It's just me.

SAM And your mum and dad?

MELANIE Just me and Mum.
There is a long pause.

SAM Hey, Ben, guess what? Melanie's as mad about football as you and Jojo!

BEN Oh great! We play after school in the park some nights.

MOUSE Yeah. Come and join in.

MELANIE Oh, thanks. Maybe. If Mum lets me.
Another long pause.

BEN Well, get on with the caption cards then!

MOUSE Oh yeah …

MELANIE Mmmm. Hey, I just need to go and … er … go to the toilet.

JOJO Do you know where it is?

SAM Do you want us to come with you?

MELANIE No, thanks … you pointed it out to me.

Exit Melanie.

BEN She seems nice.

MOUSE A bit quiet.

SAM What do you expect – meeting *you* on her first day!

JOJO I think she's great. And she likes football!
The bell rings for the end of playtime.

Scene 3

Back in the classroom after playtime.

SAM	Those captions are really scruffy, Mouse.
BEN	Well it was hard writing out in the playground.
SAM	Stop defending him, Ben! What do you think, Melanie?
MELANIE	I think it's a really interesting space collection.
MOUSE	See! Someone has good taste round here! *Jojo screams.*
SAM	What's wrong?
JOJO	It's gone.
BEN	What's gone?
JOJO	My programme! The 1966 World Cup!
MOUSE	*(Looking under the table)* It's not here, Jojo.
SAM	Mr Hopkins, Mr Hopkins, Jojo's lost her programme!
JOJO	*(Almost in tears)* I haven't lost it. It's gone.

MR HOPKINS   Calm down, Jojo. It'll be here somewhere. Just check one more time.
Sam, Jojo, Mouse, Ben and Melanie all begin to search.

MELANIE   *(Suddenly)* Mr Hopkins, can I go to the toilet?

MR HOPKINS   Mmm. Well, we try to encourage children to go to the toilet at playtime. But, if you didn't go then, well you'd better go now. Do you know where it is?

MELANIE   Yes, Sam and Jojo showed me.
Melanie leaves and Mr Hopkins goes to check the other displays in the classroom.

SAM	That's really strange. I thought she said she went to the toilet when we were all in the playground.
MOUSE	Yeah, I thought that's what she said too.
BEN	Maybe she just wants to go again.
JOJO	*(Still upset)* It's not here. It's definitely not here. Someone's taken it.
BEN	None of us would take it. Not even for a joke.
SAM	No we wouldn't!
MOUSE	Not even me!
JOJO	Then where is it? Dad'll be really upset if I say I've lost it.
BEN	Have you looked in your bag?
JOJO	See, it's not here! *(She picks up her bag and empties it onto the table.)*
SAM	Well, if it's not in the classroom, then someone must have taken it.
MOUSE	But who?
BEN	No one in our class would do that.

SAM	But someone *(pause)* **new** to our class might. *Silence.*
BEN	What, you mean …?
MOUSE	The new girl …?
JOJO	*(Shocked)* Melanie?
SAM	Well, it's possible. Did you see the way she shot out of the room the minute Jojo said she'd lost it?
MOUSE	When? When could she have done it?
BEN	When she *said* she was going to the toilet at playtime.
SAM	She had plenty of time to come in the class and …
MOUSE	And didn't you say she loved football?
JOJO	Yeah, but …
SAM	*(Spots Melanie's bag on the floor by the table)* There's Melanie's bag. *They all stare at it.*
BEN	*(Reading Jojo's mind)* You can't look in it!
SAM	If I had super x-ray vision I could see inside the bag and …

BEN Well, you haven't!

MOUSE We mustn't look in someone else's bag, it's private property.

JOJO (*Angry*) So was my football programme!

SAM It would prove it one way or the other.

MOUSE We'd get into trouble.

JOJO But she seemed so nice!

BEN She *is* nice. Maybe there's another explanation.

SAM I say we look in the bag. What do you think, Jojo?

JOJO (*Confused*) Mmmm, I … I'm not sure.

Enter Melanie.

MELANIE	What's wrong? *They all look nervous.*
SAM	*(Being brave)* Tell her, Jojo.
MELANIE	Tell me what?
JOJO	I still can't find my World Cup Final programme.
MELANIE	Oh no. Is it under the table?
MOUSE	We've already looked.
BEN	You haven't seen it, have you, Melanie?
MELANIE	*(Slightly worried)* No. Not since you showed it to us before playtime.
SAM	Are you sure you haven't seen it since then?
MELANIE	What do you mean?

Enter Mrs Turner.

MRS TURNER   Sorry to interrupt, Mr Hopkins.
All class activity and talk stops at once.

MR HOPKINS   What can we do for you, Mrs Turner?

MRS TURNER   I just want to apologise. I've just been sorting out my desk and found this right at the bottom of a pile of folders.
Mrs Turner holds up the 1966 World Cup Final programme still in its plastic jacket.

JOJO   It's my programme!

MRS TURNER   Of course, from your display! I must have picked it up with all my things when I left earlier. Oh, I do apologise, Jojo. Even I know how important the 1966 Cup Final was. You must have been wondering where it had got to.
(She gives the programme to Jojo.)

JOJO   *(Relieved)* Thanks, Mrs Turner.
Mrs Turner starts to leave, then stops and turns around.

MRS TURNER   Oh, Melanie. How are you settling in?

MELANIE   *(Not looking at Mrs Turner)* Oh, fine.

MRS TURNER   Glad to hear everyone is looking after you.

Exit Mrs Turner.

MR HOPKINS	Mystery solved, Jojo. Great news. Now, let's get our Class Museum ready for this afternoon's visit by Class 2 who, as you know, will be full of questions. *Everyone gets busy rearranging their display.*
SAM	Look, Melanie, I'm really sorry …
MELANIE	Oh, it's all right.
SAM	But we thought you'd gone to the toilet already and …
MELANIE	I didn't go to the toilet … I went to get my inhaler.
BEN	Why didn't you say you were going to get an inhaler?
MELANIE	I don't know. I was embarrassed I guess.
MOUSE	You get asthma? I get wheezy too, but not enough for an inhaler though.
MELANIE	You're lucky, they're a pain if you forget them.
JOJO	*(To Melanie)* Friends?
MELANIE	Of course, friends.
JOJO	Brilliant! I was just getting so worked up, I didn't know what to think.

SAM   No, it's all my silly fault. I was too suspicious.

MELANIE Look, it was all a mistake. Let's forget it.

BEN   *(Changing the subject)* Hey, Melanie, what do you collect?

MELANIE Don't know. *(Pause)* Oh, yes I do, I collect … new friends!